MOSS BURNING

PREVIOUS COLLECTIONS

View from the Gazebo
Descendant

MOSS
BURNING

Poems by
Marianne Boruch

FIELD POETRY SERIES
OBERLIN COLLEGE PRESS

Library of Congress Cataloging-in-Publication Data

Marianne Boruch, 1950-
   Moss Burning / Marianne Boruch.
   (*FIELD* Poetry Series; 2)
   I. Title.

   93-085658
   ISBN   0-932440-64-9
         0-932440-63-0 (pbk.)

Oberlin College Press, Rice Hall, Oberlin College,
Oberlin, OH 44074

For Aileen Jones Taylor

1883-1969

CONTENTS

III

What do I remember
  that was shaped
    as this thing is shaped?

                    —William Carlos Williams

I

THEN

Each of us had an angel. I say that now
without doubt. What does one say
to an angel, I thought, I who
never had a thought, going home
the street suddenly unreal
with both of us walking. Ahead, the bigger boys
hurled stones and shouted. Their angels—
how to imagine their beauty
unless it be anger. Embarrassing, this secret,
belief like a boat, like an odd translation
of what one thought
an ordinary word. By Mr. Glimm's crabapple,
I made them out, three
wary creatures standing at an angle,
idly lifting off the small fruits.
I dare not speak. I dare not.
Easier to imagine old men into infants,
sand back into stone. I walked past
the Ingolias' house, Mickey out there
with his big front teeth, a nervous glaring boy—
a suicide, but that was later—kicking grass
down to dirt, into dirty clouds.
Already, late summer. On the roof, his angel
draped himself over the gable, not really a gable,
the roof rising up only a little.

THE LUXOR BATHS

Before its high red brick,
a street typical of Chicago: rusted cars
and on either side, stores
boarded up, one still selling furniture cheap
and groceries in the back, and the liquor place
too busy, though the men walked past us
slowly and alone, their new bottles
in paper sacks, and singing.
                              I suppose I thought it
a movie set. I was that young.
My friend had brought me, her father
going for decades, cutting deals
on paint in the Russian bath, and even
the hotter Turkish bath, or for the new guys
who couldn't take it, the Finnish bath
with its pure, dry heat.
He was dead three years and I thought of him,
how he must have hated Wednesdays,
Ladies Night. The bored clerk behind the grill
issued us each Ivory soap,
and to wear—a sheet and a towel
for our $1.50
then slid back to her magazine.
                              It was like Riverview, walking in,
it was the fun house, Aladdin's Castle, the narrow stairs,
and that floor, all splinters and dark dust
until a room opened—full light, and in three languages, shouts
then laughter, and rows of lockers that didn't
quite close. This place—a hundred years old,
my friend whispered, more as fact
than devotion. She'd been there, after all; she'd grown up
with someone who called out
every Monday after supper, I'm going—

meaning, the Luxor,
getting in his big car, headed south toward the Loop.
I forgot to say it was snowing. It was
February, so the wet warmth
did something fuzzy to my head.
I mean, I felt faint, not sick
or maybe it was the thought
of taking off my clothes.
                                    We undressed quickly,
and hurried the narrow sheet around us, such sheet
there was. But really, I wanted
to look at them, the women. At 19, we were the youngest,
too new, too empty, and hardly worth
the effort of a question
though I feared they'd talk to us—
worried they'd *be polite*, these women
too busy with each other
and the car wreck, and so-and-so's lousy husband,
and the horse's ass of a brother-in-law
who walked out, just like that, and Irene,
what the hell would she do now?
                                    I love my sister, Irene's
sister said, that s.o.b. We were walking
toward the Russian bath, that is, they
were walking. My friend nodded,
and we tagged along. In that webby, steamy room
she and I wore our sheets, the only ones, ten of us
on wooden benches. I wanted more
about Irene. But her sister
kept shaking, *that s.o.b.*,
until a woman got up and dragged the barrel of water
and oak leaves to the center—Snap out of it, Mel!—
flicking a branch over her head, the spray
hitting the benches, the sweating walls

—a million tiny whooshes—
for everyone to laugh.
                              I pretended not to stare
but such bodies, I had never imagined
such bodies—huge breasts and thighs, and pubic hair
in lush spreading mounds, full freckled arms;
thinner women with wonderful bellies,
one had a scar.
She just let herself go after the baby came: my mother's
short circuit for anyone
like this. Here, they stood to pour water from the barrel
holding the small bucket overhead, leaning back
suddenly languid, closing their eyes.
                              They set me
dreaming this: I was invisible.
But someone turned to me—Do you want to try it?—handing me
the bucket. They were talking, off the s.o.b. now
and onto the priest
who refused to make a sick call
for someone's uncle. Jesus, the nerve of it.
Do they expect the man to crawl to church? It was hot.
I took off my sheet—
standing there, and walked and stood
and dipped my bucket in.
                              The smell of oak, soaked that way,
vaguely sweet and bitter, nothing
like pine. I wanted
to turn my back to them but didn't, lifted
the thing high
over my head to pour. I thought
of the cold outside, and the snow,
and that long blur
of anything
when it first comes down.

DRIVING AFTER SUPPER

The old senselessness returns
when driving in June
the ribbon roads, low corn
on either side, then woods, then meadows
where sheep just stand there,
slowly turn their heads. We are talking again
about how cool it is.
It could be Maine, I say
for the 20th time, though usually
this seems the other
harder world—Indiana—
birds with their *wait wait wait* high
in trees, and such hot dust
when we stop, so studded with gravel.
We pass an old brick school—1880—
disguised as someone's house, the door open
to its ring of chairs
around the small TV, a blue jacket
hung on a hook. Gifts
at every moment, though not
the farmer, farther on,
out circling in his tractor
furious haywire turns; nor the kid
at the next house who spits
on his knife, and lifts it up, quietly now
gouging the porch railing.
We barely see that, joy
being what it is, and the evening
so temporary.

RARE OLD VIOLINS

One is my neighbors' and they hang it
high above their fireplace, a stunned
baby, fine hair and inlaid tooth
and anyway, we say *ribs* and *neck* and *belly*
and touch it as if
it could talk back, however senselessly or sadly,
exactly like music.
               I walk over, afternoons,
and think of my mother's violin made for her
in her father's one brief fall of wealth. Unimaginable—
a violin made especially for a child—and how, years
later, I held it to my body, this
other body, neck and ribs,
and back arched in its nubbed parquet
spinning out. A spine.
               My son's at play, inventing
whole lifetimes with their daughter. These
five-year-olds could be thirty-five the way
they talk a subject up and down, diligently, like people
who take the stairs on purpose.
Today, it's "Orphans"—how that's exactly
what they are, and this the breathless
minute they discover. Should they sell their last
violin for bread? With mother, father dead,
do they have a choice?
               Reasonable, I think,
standing in the doorway to fetch him home, and we're
all peering up at the rare old violin. Maybe
it will reveal itself
right here, like a moon startled
to eclipse.
               But what is it, to choose? Violin
for bread, bread for violin. The children stare

and stare—such longing!—first each other, then back
to the mute violin. In some half-lit room, full
of years, two centuries ago, which ache
was which, and which was music?

THE BERLIN WALL, 1966

In Biology, the old bucket of snow melted
and got off to steam on the radiator—
distilled water for cheap, we said, the nun
at the front of the room muttering
her ancient misfortunes: a Chicago winter, the winding stairs.
That was the spring
most of us sucked our pipettes too hard
and swallowed the hay infusion
and thought we would die. All the while, in sweet litany
Margaret Woodson swore
he'd show, her German boy "bopping over the wall"
to take her to the sophomore dance.
Still we readied slides
with hair and blood, and stared
those weeks into enlargements of our tiniest selves.
The glory of God, girls! our teacher cheered and harped
over any bright bit—a fingernail, or piece of scab
down to its cellular tweed.
He got over the wall all right. Listen, such letters—
we couldn't help ourselves, Margaret said a week
before the dance, but oh my God, shot down by guards.
She told two of us this
over something fetal, a piglet maybe
or a tiny stillborn cat, cool and bluish
and so peculiar on the table, her *oh* and *oh my God* until—
poor liars—we faked our sorrow as perfectly
she faked grief.
But the ambition of it, history the least of it—those guards
we invented anyway, brutal as fathers,
and the lover, and the distant wire.
It was a table scarred for years
by bored and quiet girls. For a moment

I believed her. I remember one of us
had a knife, the other
a hand-held light.

SNOW

Cars do their deliberate absolutions
privately, in the street, grinding
gears, engine whine
and chant. Snow is
prayer rug, nothing more. And that smoke
curls and rises over wheel
and fender, the look of a moment
so openly lost.

But it might end up
in letters, the kind shrugged off,
scrawled on a postcard, one line
of pure attention. Then
it's business to be about, morning
leaking into the final
watercolor of sleep,
a blue wash, barely visible
on such fine snow.

Awake to a new planet! Is it possible
to live like this, glad
for the least treasure? The way
lit houses look, far off. Or one winter
the way the lake froze
solid as window, huts suddenly

everywhere and odd, ghosting
the ice. They weren't
prayer tents, but the men called
to the fish. I heard them: smoke
rising from their mouths.
I saw them: glittering lines descending
into the nether world. Such praise.

FOR EMILY DICKINSON

When I stood for a moment
in that white room, vines busy outside
at the screen, I thought
of the moth in you, the rich wool
it desired. I watched it
circle once, twice, nearing
the narrow bed, the little desk
though nothing was diminutive.

And I knew what a lousy daughter knows,
those years ago I lived
not three blocks from your house—idiot child,
bone stubborn, never reading your poems much, never
keeping proper vigil. Regret has its
own insect life, that tedious hum
trapped in the head. It can't get out.

But your house was too high, set on a knoll,
a wedding cake crusted
with legend. Here, eat some, my teachers said.
Each one of them would marry you. Still, once
walking past, I invented flowers
for your garden: the dumb, sweet heliotrope, the dull hiss
of lupine, delphinium's brooding reach.
Among them, you stood right up
and squinted. You who noticed everything
made nothing of me, one of the stupid
and unborn, not even the color
of a leaf yet.

Matty, here's freedom, you told
your niece one ordinary day, locking the door of that room
behind you, locking both of you in.

My aunt once gave me such a box, a nest
of boxes really, all rushed wooden birds
and fish in a tangle, all intricately carved,
each opening into its secret smaller self.
I lost count quickly. Or maybe
there were seven. I looked up,
too amazed to tell her.

THE BOY GHOST

For years we weren't children exactly
but small birds, our look
almost intelligent, as though the long hallways
could be maneuvered as easily as trees
any afternoon. Slow, that classroom, full
of arithmetic and thick lead
in pencils. Slow the door
as it opened to the
quick crying hinge—no one touched it, I swear—
the nun in her billowing black—
Children, Robert's come—the chalk
mid-air, her arm raised
like a saint's in a picture. The sky outside,
cloud and dark and thunder there.
                              Straight ahead we looked
and drifted, trained to love our secrets
so secretly. But to watch her eyes
was to watch him moving—
the boy ghost, slow motion, taking his time
past the high bookcase, past our little desks, poor thing
all-made-of-light, poor thing
in that old woman's head that refused to lose itself
out the small leak in her memory
where everything else was going: the names of things,
our names.
                    Spring, and so many windows open
in spite of the storm. Which one
would the dead boy choose? What shape
is a ghost or an angel? This lens
he would slip through to fly invisible and perfect and huge—
we believed nothing and we
believed this, equally; the forsythia

quietly dashing its yellow fringe
against screen and glass.
Our teacher stood there,
she hadn't moved.

                        Such wind, the trees
bent with it.

THE KINGDOM

Long afternoons in bed, we loved
to talk about the woman
on the el, remote
as a rabbit and that intense,
who froze at every stop
until the train
leapt up and knocked us back.
But she'd
lunge forward in her seat,
pedal in a fury
we never biked with, even uphill
or after dark, while the thing wheezed
and clanked and roared on
to the next station.
She'd ease as the speed let up,
sucking air like a swimmer, shrinking down
to her curious deadpan.

Our room floated then, nearly
out its window
at anything so strange, your arm relaxed,
cool across my belly.
We'd think of her—that woman
wild again, that
whole train back, rattling off
its *here* and *here*
and *henceforth*: Lincoln Avenue, Armitage,
Oak Street's dazzling deadend beach.
Not ours, of course.
Of course, hers. Or so
she thought, glaring *ingrates* at us once
in some station's high-dive calm,

ennobling herself
for the next great surge.

An unmade bed for days, that bed,
dusk settling like sugar turning a water glass
sweet and murky. We thought of her
a lot, the way we wondered
everything: not love exactly, not that, more
what that woman saw, say,
when released, she
looked down at her kingdom—
sure, those obvious streets, but such alleys,
glittering and twisting....

THE JUNKED CARS

Maybe it wasn't the cars so much
but that click in the head that comes in fall—
the five or six of us somewhere
in our twenties walking out of woods
into sudden light—the pasture!
And there and there and there, those
elegant gods in their blue-black ruin
up on blocks, or rusting sideways
into their running boards, tires
half-rotted off their rims. Say *1933*, and our parents
still stunned kids—the ghost
of kids in those high back seats. It began
to snow a little. Car after car, we wedged ourselves
behind the steering column, and through the windshield's
splintered daze, saw the woodline rise and flash—maples
and oaks just past their brilliant flagging, whirling now
in the shattered glass, hundreds
of separate visions, deranged
and at rest.

So we shot the whole afternoon. None of us
had children yet, or real jobs
to carry on our backs like loam, that secret
creature life in every fifth grade text, moving
those insects to move the earth, bit
by fragrant bit. Such hard-shelled hope, enormous
and primeval—the cars wheezed and groaned
with us inside. We rolled windows down,
peered across the battered hoods.
No roads, of course. Whoever drove there
drove straight through woods. So we
kept at it, walking home—the picture of it—takes

and sad retakes and into evening.
Lovely virus—*wonder*—as it works its way
into the body, dark
as darkness fills a house, the porch light off,
the moon up, but barely half itself.

WORK

Chicago—and the days of the terrible job,
the terrible ride to work above neighborhood
and neighborhood, every window below
caught in the same torn curtain, or so it seemed
from the El, a thing dizzy with its own
volts and brakes. I pressed my cheek
against the glass and kept looking: even the flashing
backyards turned ancient, each
almost a square, pinned down with a chair
tilted backward or broken. How long is anyone
twenty-three or four—endless moment
dragged through its bored cousins. *Years*.

And my job: papers into files, files
into their buzzing slots, day after day
at the great university. Near Christmas, nothing
much to do, my office mate hummed
as she sewed and folded ornaments, her desk
an acre of sequins and ribbon. I typed
deep into the early twilight—poems—and stared
them through. Poor things. It was like walking
sideways into the massive heart—a heart
as big as a room—at the Museum of Science and Industry,
following the dim light
in the blue-pitched veins, that gun barrel
double rap in my head. Someone's
real heart, the guide said, amplified one hundred times.

Coming home, I'd see the old man
severed at the waist, and walk by quickly.
Each day he'd set up at the El, his odd little chair,
his can of frosted ballpoint pens. I once

bought two. Pretty soon—I don't know.
I quit before long. By then, it was summer.
The half-man in his tee shirt
began to balance bottle
onto bottle into a glittering, threatening lace.
Look out, he'd say, rolling
back on his ball bearings the size of a fist,
careful of us, loving our danger.

SPRING

In your deliberate dark despondence, thick as syrup
and as rich, spring descends
like an afterthought, dizzy rapture, trick.
So I left you
in the living room, and walked carefully
to the barn, over mud,
over boards we threw down
for paths, this trespass to the heart.
It was afternoon, late, the last
of March. Or it was early evening
when the brain shuts down to any thought
but supper. Then the sawdust where you cut
our winter wood, I saw it
rotting everywhere, old seepage
all autumn, the scent of foul decay.
So this is spring, I thought, standing there.
A sparrow swooped above me
in the loft. I could hear
its small body grazing beams and windows,
knew its anxious chatter, its
ridiculous ascent. Thirst
for the shaft of light bringing down
what is possible, thirst for everything
undiscovered, all the what ifs
passing like wings
into the next day and the next.

TOTAL ECLIPSE

Don't look at it, my grandmother said.
So I dragged the big box with its pinhole
upright and over me
next to the garden.
All shade in there,
the raw scent of cardboard, the feel
of July like fur.
I waited in my dumb animal doze, watched
the point of light on the inside wall
narrow and cut back
oblong to arc, a sliver of moon, this sun before
darkness took
the whole box with it. Not fast though,
slow as a mile in such heat,
as a girl walking it
with nothing in her head.
But night flooded everywhere
the brilliant afternoon had been.
I raised the box to see it, color faded from the garden,
blood gone out of the roses. I could tell
flowers, merely thicker
than the vines.
So hot—
I lay down in the grass,
bearable now, night
such as it was, cooler, dark,
and the house a dense looming thing,
not so far. I thought
of my grandmother inside. I thought
why doesn't she turn on a light.
You'll go blind,
she had said. Don't you
look at it. But weeks I'd invented it—flame

spinning clean
out of a coin so hot
you seared fingers back to bone
just thinking.
        I see the child I was,
stupid, sitting up, lying back again.
A cricket now and then, tentative,
confused. I half-heard him
where weeds began, all prickles
and tiny blooming knots
closing
because they were fooled.
        Then it was simply dusk.
A day of it. An hour.
And the moon between the sun and the earth
was a hand on my forehead, a human
voice at my ear.

WINTER

In winter, the kitchen is this pre-dawn gift:
the chipped enamel stove
almost a thought itself after years, there
in the corner dreaming
its next life: not a refrigerator, no,
a red sports car.
But we'd be the old aluminum coffee pot,
faithful and indifferent both,
shrugging off the pride of a charred handle.
Half-asleep, I take the thing these days
and fill it up, and set it down again,
measure and measure the coffee, heaped now
to a dark fragrant shape
until the kitchen's held up, a blue-tipped match,
this moment raised, before striking.   I mean

for hours it's been like this—snowing.

PAINTING FERNS
A MILE FROM THE STADIUM

Difficult to get it right
the foliage
in its complicated grief.
So one gives up right off
and paints instead what is half
imagined, half kept secret all these years
in the flippant, industrious hand.
How watercolor leaps, and each frond
comes quickly now against
the steady afternoon, the ticking chiming clock
locked in dense mahogany.
Beyond, it's trees
in their old disguise of rapture, pointed
reds, delinquent yellows. They lash the eye.
The fern on paper
is equally improbable, though there
it floats, and wills its
own ghost life. I narrow
like a surgeon to add blue to the stem.
The leaf flares out again
in shadow. *Mystery,*
until the room is that much dimmer, the distant
cries quick, animal,
thousands at the stadium rising
and falling in their seats
as if wounded.

TOWN POOL

Children bobbing there—
of course they should be dizzy
but they're dreaming the boat's sunk
and the shore recedes, and this
brief life's all theirs, this
once, twice
under the blue water
until someone bumps them, and they sputter
and thrash and it comes to them
here they are, only seven, not far
from supper, their
ordinary beds.

Afternoons, the mothers
lie back alone, or gossip idly on benches.
They don't own these children.
They don't own each other.
Some read a book
whose lurid cover is as accurate
as the way the children
pretend not to be children
but the ageless brilliant who survive,
who let love
burn their lives.
The pool invites that sleepy
double ache all summer, the hill,
past the cyclone fence,
so high and green above the water.

One might look down from there,
the pool no mirror
but frenzy, that vacant blue—

how passion works: urgent, then casual,
then urgent. The brave shouts of the children
belie the inner secret children.
And of the mothers who
lie or sit so still, with
their word or two—one stirs, her hand raised
to shade her eyes. Great change
comes like this.

MAPS

Those days we had no maps.
I would walk home from anywhere and find it.
The house was something high
as though hundreds of leaves, none identical,
buoyed it up, an offering
above the street, backfiring trucks, damaged
neighbors intent on the next
dark wish. We heard them
humid nights, Miss Starr
in the next apartment, falling over chairs, yelling
get out of here all of you. Get out
of here. Clunk, bang,
then silence. She was past 60, and we
shy as that creature part
of the moon eclipsed by earth, paced
our small adjoining porch, wondering who we were
to do things. You hiked over
the railing, inched along the gable, her kitchen
a few steps more. *Miss Starr?* Sprawled backwards, alone,
she just looked at you, senator for the whole
dumb planet. You too, she said
in elegant burn, and turned away.

That was years ago, and what right have I?
Miss Starr could be dead by now, and the house, who knows,
full of earnest, optimistic strangers.
But you, climbing back that night
into our tiny place, those lines in you
—such secrets in the body—I could follow them down
to the world's first sorrow, and drown myself
as simply as a child might, her parents
barely out of earshot. In that half dark, we stood
and listened at the wall, untangling kindness

from the map of kindness, until
normal sounds returned—a bath being drawn, drawers
opening and closing—and the years
began their clockwork.

NEIGHBORHOOD ROOFS

All summer, so many roofs
torn off and put back—one
three story I biked by,
so steep, the men hanging there by ropes.
Here, one sang, *here*, pointing to a place
past lathe, into simple posts
and beams before I, quick,
turned the corner
and lost it.

It's just that
watching roofers from my kitchen once
I saw the old man we hired
move so lithely
on our garage—tearing off and putting back,
for days, the blunt unhurried hammer.
I watched his granddaughter
up there too, though
they never spoke. She put on earphones
and across and down the incline
moved to music. She painted her hammer
blue. Sometimes, raised,
it vanished into the sky's
same color. I walked out one time
and shouted up—water? lunch?
But they didn't want anything,
looking down at me like some dim
distant stars, the night
too cloudy.

Roofers are crazy, a carpenter told me.
I think of the rope that held
those men, the light and air

flooding into that attic
after a century of dark.
To be up there, to invite a house
back to its x-ray,
to the few beams it was—
they must dream everything wrong,
in reverse, and be
glad of it, stripping down
past that first wish to be something
to the deeper one, to be
nothing, before giving up
and building back.

ON SORROW

The way certain people
run through rain at rest stops, the quiet ones
or the quick shrieking ones,
is the way I want
to think about sadness: brave flash
and the weedy grass too shiny in such light,
say, the middle of September
which is always at a slant, the kids
already school-dogged, hitting
every puddle, that slow motion rush
from the car.

But it's the stranded ones there,
old guys with caps, a woman
with her hood up—I look at them
and hardly think at all.
They stand whistling for their genius dogs, dogs
who half-fly
through the dog walk zone. Two notes
to that whistling, or three.
Each has a rhythm I can't quite get.
They hunch down
into their nylon jackets, shoulders
already dark with rain.
I don't know
what it is—just what you do
if you have a dog, like
it's raining all day, regardless.

Half the time, I sit a few minutes
in my car before
I do anything. One of them is always trying

to light a cigarette
in the rain. Match after soggy match
flung down. This is hope.

MOSS BURNING

All night and day through summer the peat field
glowed, and turned us back to our lives, these bodies
rattling around the old house
burning quietly, microscopically, just
picking up a cup or going out
to check the mail. I drove there.
I mean I wanted to. Twice the morning paper gave itself
to neighbors fed up with smoke, their clothesline clothes
thick with it, their windows
shut all day, terrible in such heat.
The farmer shrugged: just clearing.
But it wouldn't quit. And then
that breathlessness when a few small fires
jumped water—that ditch flooded
deep around the field to contain it—now
slowly searing the bedraggled corn or another's wheat.

But it was night that concerned me,
how the low moss must look under the clear drought-struck
stars, a kind of idle indifferent burning, as if some
weird lower-depth sea life had come
with their little head lanterns, and taken root amid the twisted
vegetation, slicks of flame
in the billowing rows, quick
as synapses sparking nerves.

Perhaps it was our feverish boy, crying out
don't, and turning in his bed
like old machinery, not quite catching, or you
asleep in your exhaustion, open-mouthed, astonished
at the inner planet. But just then I dreamt it,
dreamt the car stalled there at the field.
It was cool for a change. I sat on the hood

and considered Orion still pinned in winter
under the horizon somewhere, the field
crossing and recrossing
its luminous radar, flash points
in the dark before speech.

That hush—not one word, nothing of deliberate lifetimes.
I could have been a kid gone blank with agony
or joy, leaning back against
the borrowed Chevy, breaking curfew
that ordinary summer before Kennedy was shot.
Or back of that, just a child lifted up on the hood,
squinting into the family photo, caught there
black and white, in a moment
I'll never remember. As if looking through such twilight
you could forget something. As if you
could put on sunglasses of the darkest sort, and turn
into some young man at Los Alamos, say,
in his sunglasses, crosslegged
and cocksure on the hood—a G.I. jeep
or some beat-up Plymouth—bongo drums
between his knees, poised for the poisonous seizure
of light, the torn retina.
We see through that eye. We close it
to sleep.

Snow, said the paper next. That would put the field out.
It's fall. Each morning now
the children lope toward the yellow bus,
my son among them, until they vanish.
The street goes silent then, as if
they were never born.
But it's burning,

acre on acre, no break in that fury—
so close to here—
too much of the invisible, visible.

II

TREE

Its disguise was ugliness, and ants
in cheap parade, up and across,
and electric wires cut
right through at a heartless angle
to keep Walter Cronkite on at the neighbors'
so proud of their TV.
                        Thick, thick as too much
of too many summers is thick,
three and a half kids to get human arms
around it.
            In the dark, it rose up
like the drawing of a tree a girl might make
to scare her mother.
                        I was there. I was almost asleep
but the moon—or was it a porch light
left on all night?
What I didn't know
is what I still don't know,
                        that one loves
ugliness as one loves beauty,
which is to say, how the dead love
because they've given up on love: *the ants?*
okay, really—broken branches? fine, fine....

THE STAIRWAY

Once in a houseful, against everything
elusive and too loud, I kept
the smallest solitude.
I could cup my hands and see it, that flame
a brief blue. Which is to say
I was twenty, dragged along—of course, a party—
my roommate had a new
wild boy, remote and sweet, those two,
as another species. Believe this:

we said nothing, crosslegged on the floor.
But my god—one second
just a wall before us, whole and blank,
it flashed open to a stairway,
stairs in the nowhere upward gloom like some great
bad movie, some
changeling's breathless launch.

I turned to my friend—do you see that stairway?—
who grinned at her friend: *Gerard,*
she sees the stairway.
Such racket parties make—in every other room, laughter,
bodies slow and quick with each other,
and that god-awful music.

Is it fair to say now I dreamt this
years ago, woke up
still twenty, amazed at the nonchalance
of certain mysteries: my roommate sleeping, the curtains
stunned with light. And in this quiet, half
a lifetime now. That dream
is twenty.

Outside it's early, and into
a final decade. It's summer, too warm

for morning, the air like something
someone already breathed in.

I breathe it in, who knows whose spirit.

• • •

If I could dream again like that, turn it over
as we used to hold
an ailing bird in one hand, an eyedropper
careful in the other,
would the dead begin to speak?
Its tiny mouth opens exactly
like a hinge, as each same chamber
of the heart unlocks, unlocks.
Even of things we love, what remains?
Of summer, say, one image maybe—a car,
a gravel road
too little for the map, how
one of us stopped arguing, violent at the gears
backed up to see that deer alone
and slow, right
at us in the field, chewing the soybean's
ordinary leaf.

All pause is ancient though minutes
speed like light. Forget *coming from*
or *going to*, a story
breaks to threads, worn down by details
until the last detail floats
like a stick in water, two sticks.
That deer we save
for when the room gets dark, his curious look, or how young
he was, stupid, an easy shot
in growth that low, or the wide-brimmed leaf

—this stays—oh, each
bigger than his tongue.
The field shrinks then billows up.
One's lithe
and seasick with it.

       • • •

Not that we could go there. Not that we could
leave this body like a thing
hanging on a hook, and enter like an angel.
Far easier to say
what is beautiful to say, that fields release
their silence like a scent, that any pasture
fenced and distant, haunts
like some pure creature out of Euclid.
The horizon's drugged by that. And years,
his book of perfect shapes, it's open
on a desk until
the cool-tipped pointer in our teacher's hand
glints again like something
launched through air, and shatters.
Dearest ones, she says
not sweetly, is it this? or this?

One makes *story* from what broken bits
one has. Of course the nun was old,
past 80, those lines and angles hers completely.
Give them back! We did,
good repentant thieves, tongue-tied
with guessing. Every hallway darkens then dimly
lights itself.
I ached like that—to mess things up
and be sincere. Once after class
I seized the chalk, pressed

my oddball squares
and squiggles. Can we prove these, Sister?
Maybe universal laws for these?
Those, she said, they're nothing. Get them off the board.
My nothings, off—off!—my next-
to-nothings. But their manic outlines stayed
next morning, faint map
to shame and joy, two tiny kingdoms linked
by the narrow bridge I stood on.
I still vote
from that bridge; a sometime worthy citizen, I guard it
with my ferocious shrug.

But this dream of strangeness
has a slower scarecrow life. Now I hear it
another way: kids this morning flood the porch, they're true
and funny both. I want their wires, their
flashing discontent with stillness.
They fight to be the dead guy in the play
until the winner throws her body on the porchswing.
No way, they cry. You can't laugh.
You're dead. You can't.

• • •

We hug that fact as though the dead
were always in lament. It makes us the only ones
to be so happy. Don't swear to it.

This first: you have an uncle,
disappeared for years who dies
an old man but you dream him
young that week, bathrobe-young, the thing
slipping off his shoulder.
He's too radiant to care.

Second, I'll take him back—no pretense—
my uncle then, and I tell him outright in the dream
how good he was, a good uncle.
But I haven't seen you in 20 years, he almost sings.
So what, I say. It was the idea
of you—the opera you loved, the novel you wrote
then burned when you came back from war.
Oh, that. He's laughing, so graceful
in the blousy bathrobe, flushed
with sudden circumstance. Will you come
to visit us? I say. I know it's far, this house
in Maine. *Maine?* he says. *Maine?*
—arms sweeping toward the loosest heaven—
My dear, I can do anything—jubilant, triumphant—*I'm dead!*

Whitman, ghost-to-be
when he wrote his glad insistence
on any beauty, that "to die
is different from what any one supposed,
and luckier"—as if such luck
could free a life
from its saddest nowhere, as if one's crystal ball
looked back.

My dream believes him though, an old man new,
and raised, and roaring, still
one of us. Uncle, after years
I'm dizzy with it, getting up again
in that day's cold light, in that house
we've sold and left, not sure
what besides your happiness
is waking. Just *one of us, one of us*—weird
lovely warp passing
through the stubborn body to its darkest pinpoint:
Tod Browning's film—remember?—six

decades old, *Freaks*, that
little jewel
caught sideways in the throat. It's hard
to breathe.

But in college—forgive me—all my housemates
rushed to be disfigured
and demented, the mutilated, the misjudged,
the film's poor lyric folk
outside the building on the quad where
someone kept it showing. Extra credit for Psychology?
Practical Endocrinology? For Entomology? Really, we looked
a child's idea of insects, shadowed
in the bushes against the show's finale
to leap into spring's sweet dark
and chant the famous chant: *we accept you, google gobble,*
one of us, one of us, bearing down
on those little Gidget moviegoers our screwed-up
homemade masks, our all-embracing arms, so many, like some
awful Shakti.

Who were we in those twilight seconds?—ancient something
hissing in the moonlit inner ear.

And of the stairway dream? Some dreams are our reward
for cowardice or secrets, the way
we fly, or love completely. But none of us rose
to walk those steps.
Dear Uncle, not one of us, one of us
that luminous or brave.

• • •

So every night we walk real stairs, my son
once so carefully
chanting the litany of the netherworld—his *bad dreams?*
to my *no, good ones.* His *bad dreams? bad?*
to my cheerful hopeless *good* and *good* and *good.*
Safe to sleep then. Safe.
And the room is any room, all gauzy streetlight shape
taking its ruin
calmly, willfully to dawn.
Of course birds again. But we forget
what they are—old dinosaurs
shrunk down
centuries of morning
to whatever bearable size.

WALKING HOME

Good Friday then,
March, the month to remember nothing
though some of us try—
crocus, and the tiny iris, perfect memories they have
coming up the same way, out of god-knows-where,
the bleak lush bottom of things.
                              It's the high sweet gloom
of church, this air,
late afternoon on the street, all the flowers going inward,
not anything like sleep. Lamps on in the houses,
one after another until the moon
is just the next lit window
hung high overhead.
                    Good flowers, I say to their darkness, good
walking up the steps.

THE SPIDER

I know spiders watched us. So I lay too still
in the cabin, listening, you
making your way to the one light bulb
hung from the bathroom ceiling,
so careful with the door
not to wake me.

The whole time I thought of the moon
kept part secret by cloud, and how you said
what's that? to the locusts and cicadas
and that single cry, far off in woods.
Our bodies told us the difference,
our nerves and blood
more accurate than memory.

One spider took the beam above us.
I tried to watch her in the dark.
At dawn, waking first, I saw
her swift and mindful crossing, one line
over the others, under and over again, a weave
made of hours and the thinnest light.

But beauty is danger, a web. It rose and fell
with your sleeping, breath in
and out. All of it she rode fixed, like some
lunar tide. What was I looking at
to stare straight at her? Things rest
or they wait.

ASH WEDNESDAY

Only vines still loop and twist
and fill the arbor. Grapes—the few
missed by squirrel
and bird—went inward months ago,
shrunk ancient to seed
as they float there.
                        All afternoon then
shears and a rake, the little cart
piled high three times now, every worthless
branch and stem
loved too much last summer.
                                        I'm slow as a year at this.
Gooseberries, lilac,
clematis back to the flowering wood.
I stand on the brink so long
it's nearly prayer: dear thing in the ground,
sleeping thing, thing dreaming itself
black with frost. I can't think
I do it right. I
can't think.
                    It's cut above the bud. It's
cut at an angle, always. It's
cut the odd branches
that will touch, and tangle out light
when the deep leaves come.
Such a dutiful daughter: I do
what the book says, almost.
                                    But I hardly believe
the deep leaves will come. It's warm
for February, for early March—whatever
month this is.
I bring a radio out here. I set it up
like a god in the garden.

GEESE

They open their beaks and something comes out—
a long ribbon.
And nothing to do with fear, what
they see up there.
It's like breathing to them
to swoop and glide,
a full bellows in those bodies
gives out a great foghorn.
A boat too lost in the water
might mistake it
for rescue, and signal hopelessly
with a flag, that flag
once a shirt.
To them, such a tiny flapping thing below
on the blue expanse
is—
no, not a wing.
Still their fine broad voices circle
and come down.
Oh heart of the world
briefly,
as the heart is pierced.

III

UP IN AIR

the plane's all insect intelligence,
the drone and spit of it
in the girls' murmuring three rows up:
the class trip
to Salt Lake. In a minute, they'll
rise and take pictures of each other, shooting
goofy or sweet,
whatever self-consciousness brings
in its instant, stilled bouquet.

Miles below, farms
but no one's working them.
A gate hangs on one hinge, geese land
hundreds at once, in trees.
Don't listen to this. Romance—
half lie, half wish. Not a fencepost
is visible. Up here, one imagines it.

I mean, even the baby beside me
is all blank curiosity, rattling
his keys. Dumb luck
for the dentist and his dentist friend,
and their wives across the aisle—
Oh bountiful country
of a billion rotting teeth.
And now, the tired stewardess is here
and here and here. She's
all business, she's blurry.
Whatever's secret
remains secret, furious years
come to nothing
in this low white noise. But surely

everyone's had a childhood.
And that lake back there

where someone drowned,
and the gate
hanging crooked, and the geese,
well, they're sad too,
and ancient and brand-new.
The coffee cart, it barely fits
the narrow aisle
and the dentists shine, so happy
with decision: cream or not, sugar?
no sugar. One invents
and lying back, uninvents: *Dissolve*
Return   Do not assume.

Below us, by now—Utah.
Below Utah, molten ore.
And still the plane—that roar is constant,
meaning fragile, meaning
about to change.

ARGUMENT, WITH MIGRATION

By Radioville, we were impossible, though the cranes,
they were radiant. They couldn't have cared less.
So many thousands the sky
blacked out: worse than inkblot, worse
than the school nurse, all business, pointing, now

what does this suggest to you? *Suggest.*
We'd got to the woods by then, and their voices
collapsed around us, hideous, like plastic
scraping plastic raw, amplified
by every heartsick turning leaf. Yet these were
real birds, big
strange ones, flamingo maybe, grayed out
by ancient circumstance, and awkward
as they landed, folding up like flimsy aluminum
chairs left out all fall
in the overgrown yard. Wind could
snap them in two, like that.

I was careful not to look at you, and held
the binoculars high until the world
narrowed and got bigger, the cranes
deliberate as monsters, lovable as any clumsy thing.
They never stopped talking.
But how private it was, their descent into the bleak
marsh, cornstalks bent back to a spirit self,
so far from summer. I turned

to look at you, binoculars
still in place. I fiddled with the lens: you
blurred, not blurred. You blurred again and again
as the birds dimmed into
twilight, quieting, dozing off,
whatever they do.

IN SUMMER

The way old men sometimes
cast their lines, and recast them off the city docks,
all morning the light just so,
the thread flaring up
to cross the sky to water—I could be
that asleep, or in some slow canoe
and beyond, a band is really playing, practicing
so badly you can barely catch how it stops
and starts again, and every time
much worse.   So a canoe rocks exactly
this certain dream-like way, the paddle laid across
and birds above in their haughty
quarrel—which one will eat?—but all of them
are overweight, too fat to fly, all belly
as they circle lower.   How long have I
been like this? I have one shoe on
and one shoe off, the kids outside
making an ordinary street of it, how they shout
and laugh and complain—no fair!—
until lungs break.   By afternoon, maybe one guy's
left, reeling out his line, pulling
the damn thing in. No hope in it, the hand,
but sullen joy. The band is getting softer—they
must be marching off—their careful, awful music
high as harps, and blocks to go.

THE SURVEYING CLASS

The young men on a yellow day with lines
and scopes surveying off
the minutes and the corner as cars
crowd past, mute as grand events
that went before—armistices, moon missions,
Charlemagne's last idiot move: this is

a class. We're just walking by. One kid
straddling a fence cries out like a maiden in the tale.
He gets a lot of laughs.
Clerkly wit, you say, going on about something
on the gravest of star charts.

In the mob of students, we hear a young woman:
I just don't think about him anymore. That's it.
And her friend nods dimly.
Always this studied nonchalance. Now they're both
not thinking about him, sure.
And he's elsewhere, not thinking about her either.

Around us, even the trees
are dizzy with lies in every color.
This is fall. We get
used to it: pose, revelation, pose.

DISTANCE

The boy swimming, barely swimming, holding on
to the styrofoam raft, thinking he's swimming,
swimming through his childhood like that, thinking
he's doing something—swimming—
                              Now a grown man,
someone else in the lake's
calm center, his boat nearly swamped,
tipping over. The man barely holds the whole business
upright, thinking he's almost there, if only,
thinking yes, this is sailing, thinking he's sailing,
sailing through his adulthood like that, thinking he's
doing something—sailing—
                              Meanwhile, stones over years
lose themselves to sand, and storms
take down trees limb by limb. Birds
are this clear: you hear them
before you see them—
                              Standing there, with my binoculars,
the world caught quick, thinking
this is seeing something: a jay in the elm, the man
sailing, the boy hardly visible
in a lifetime of water, thinking I'm really doing
something, the detail
at such distance—

AT THE Y

In the pool with huge fish on the wall,
light there, and that chlorine blue,
the old women grabbed
the sides and walked all winter
up and down the water, one
with a tube up her nose and taped there,
one with a neck brace,
shrunk delicate as a child, and others—
I can't remember how many.
                          I'd watch their thin backs
breathe as they walked away.
I'd squint
from the skylights. Even a sigh
had an echo there, that sweet water
an eye with no
brain behind it to speak of.
                          They'd smile at me,
so exhausted in the locker room.
They'd smile as they
came toward me through the water
where I stood
and fiddled with my goggles, always
fogged up. Above us
the lifeguard was a high eclipse, in earphones,
his eyes rolled sideways, his body
barely holding in
another body that swayed and whirred
and wouldn't come back.
                          But I'd dive down
to a deeper nothing, pale
as pale jelly, the kind with no flavor
just the smallest scent. I got so
I'd forget the whole business
in the same tired gesture my arms would make,
the long weight I carried

thinning out to the sound of blood
in my head, that pastoral.
                              It wasn't music,
it wasn't anything at all, only
the going and the coming and the going,
the hard breath between.
I could leave it quick. After so long, I'd
pitch backward against the side
and hang there. We wake from the dullest dreams
that startled way, and lie
down again in the dark.
                              I'd lift my blind goggles—
the boy guard folding towels now, quiet,
bored with his misery. But those women
taking it so patiently, up and down the shallow end
where danger was
exact and unending.

PIANO

Late night, and we talked you
into another lifetime with its lights
turning up just
when you stood to play
that terrible piano, creature off
by years of weather,
dampness like distraction, like love,
which takes out bone and breath, and puts it back
so crooked. But this wasn't the body,
the chilly, woozy sound
you whirred out, though it took us
down and up and finally elsewhere
in its intricate meander.
It killed you to play notes
so long out of key,
going tinny in any riff
though I loved those
odd seconds—the only doors I could enter,
the endearing spots
full of *anyway*, and *in spite of*
and *what the hell*
as you kept going. I thought
of your music teacher then, the taut,
excitable man you spoke of, pulling you out of class,
and the gym where you
sat with him, duet after duet, years
—real music, you said, not like this.
But mainly, it was that cavernous room
I couldn't leave, its great drifts
of air and light, the high
bare bulbs in cages, those windows
to be opened awkwardly
with a long hooked stick.

DR. WILLIAMS' DESK

is, of course, all clutter pinned
loosely down—the crooknecked lamp, the window,
so light returns by accident
and by design. The chair is one of those worthy
wooden jobs, fluid on its narrow pivot, the bared
bald-eagle wheels. Carpet, some watery flowers
fading out of chorus
on a deadpan note. Good black and white, good
camera in its sudden shroud.
The typewriter is here, the radiator, both
objects of interior order, the steam of things,
the darkened quick. It seems morning
in this room, the windows flooded with it,
the gauzy curtains
just a gesture. Outside New Jersey and New Jersey
and New Jersey. But real place
and time—inside—I let it float
on my own choked half-light all day.
Lamp, paper, window, books: an ordinary room,
no flash, which is to say
anyone might be walking by, look in,
so *what about it*. So what. O Williams,
who knew what he knew right here.

HOLY CARDS

A miracle, how the printing press
eked out haloes, and the pious freeze
in each picture—eyes locked inward on some
luminous dot in a head gone dark
as the TV dying to its own
bright pinpoint. We found the gold-rimmed cards
left behind in pews those Saturdays
after funerals as the last
old woman struggled into her Buick
and drove off.

You and I were maybe ten, so keen
on those keepsakes, low rent relics
of the one-most-recent dead. I turned one card
over to the *b. 1902* and the *d. just three days before*
and the *dear husband, father, beloved brother*—no one
we knew—and the little prayer.
It was Polish or Italian, another planet.
Creepy, you said. Come on. Sad tickertape, they were
mostly scattered in the back
and so many kinds: Jesus holding his pierced heart
straight out like a drugged surgeon; Mary
dizzy with visions or accidents
or both; or poor ordinary Joseph distracted
by sawdust in the shop, wielding an honest-to-god
awl as if nothing bad could happen.

By then, you were scouting near the altar,
no good unless
the men had knelt there, the kind who half-sat, leaning back,
a certain bored tilt to their heads,
and clearly still at the office or sunk
in their slow backyards in those cheap webbed chairs.
They never took cards home. You'd genuflect before
slipping down each pew—such good girls we were—then

turn and flash
a fist, thumb high. A find.

Walking home, we'd count our kill, trade
as our brothers traded a Willie Mays for an Ernie Banks.
We'd do the sappy holy look: folding our hands,
hypnotized, standing just right
between leaves
so the light would fall straight
in that single famous shaft. Those silly, sweetened,
wounded cards. But we saved them anyway,
and looked at them and looked
and laid them out
like solitaire in the quiet bedroom, those
blank ecstatic faces all
gazing back at once.

AT SCHOOL

They write and read to know everything worth knowing
each fall past snow to spring.
The yellow buses stop
and children wander off, this place a dream
their first dream
empties into. But the teachers,
so real and quick, open their trunks
to the parking lot. Woven bags they carry in,
books, bottles, all business this
early, the dim hall, dim
until they step there.

One teacher doubts herself, and the children
love that darkness.
She stands at the window
looking out so much she could be weather
or a kind of light they've seen in pictures,
scary, depending.
The room slips then, like ice
on ice. They fiddle at their desks,
walk around, know she knows at heart who
they are—fish or giant
ancient squids at sea bottom, not kids at all.
Certain moments her darkness floods
the whole room at a thing
one says by accident
or because it sounded close. They watch her
whisper back
the awkward word or phrase, whatever it is,
whatever hung in the air those twenty seconds
like a kite wounded,
coming down.

At recess, she's in there, quiet.
She's in there, I know

she is, two of them say, two
who should be out on the playground, screaming.
Not one of them moves
though they want to—oh, they want to.
It's neither happiness
nor sadness
how they lean their heads
against her door that way.

STILL LIFE AND GLOBE

Downstairs, the world's
off its axis, wrenched by our boy
and left last night
in the battered wicker rocker.
Now Antarctica's usual chilled blue stone
rides the side like any
ordinary continent, and that hot
equatorial ribbon
rises to a pole, humid bathwater
iced over.
                So we persuade
the stillborn galaxy to star, a dog
to talk romance. Upstairs, he has
no mind for this, shot through
with rigid sleep. And no one rules
that planet.

THE CRICKETS

moved their waterworld
under the piano. All fall I came down at 5 a.m.
to their sweet mad hundreds, the whole house
drowning. But each dawn ended the mindless
pull of that water, one oar and one oar and one oar—
B flat maybe if I had any sort of ear.
(My brother with perfect pitch would have turned his head,
listened like a screw to wood....)
Oh, it's hard how human they were, their bravado boring,
eternal, not like a clock though, more
ingenious than that.
Or so I heard once—
if you counted how many per minute, every whirl
and wire, halved or quartered it, minus fifteen, you'd know
love like a thick drink or death's
exact reach or which angels wait with their catapult
for the brain to go dark
as sleep is dark, as years are.
But it's always night in there surely, the body
of the cricket a brief, high explosive.
Hardly any light
but that.

WIND STORM, LATE MARCH

Poor bees, the tree down in such winds,
the gleaming criss-cross combs
in the spilt hollow.
                          Cold that morning,
the bees clustering for warmth,
stingless in the shock of it, a few
aimlessly rising, the tree splintered—
limbs and trunk in pieces
all over the street.
                          Pearl Street,
and the bees in its round yellow light
wanting only the old
darkness of the hollow, the heat
of the bark, rooting wood close enough
to bury the long flights
though, of course,
                          they do not dream.
We pretend they do, pretend they sleep
hanging there, all wings
and the hard black thousands of bodies
but that time, they were just
stunned, meaning
what now? meaning *summer, and what
use is it?*—
                          The men were coming, their
trucks and loud indifferent saws,
bits of honey and wax
to flying air. The bees—not even
angry, soothed almost
by such confusion,
                          hovering there,
hovering. What do we know of anything?
The roar of the men, the same
storm all night....

TO ALL THOSE POETS ONE READS
IN CHILDHOOD

From this distance, any crow
could be the only crow against that dopey landscape—
those good girl books, or comics fading
on each blinding back porch, our mothers
still loyal to things that blossomed
mindlessly all summer, the sweet-toothed pansy, the deliberate,
stubborn marigold. But Oliver Wendell Holmes, say,
or Edna St. Vincent Millay, or that Sara
what's-her-name Teasdale, until the last
John—himself—Masefield dropped
dead center into our land-locked state, clearly
a seizure, the way brick streets pulled back, right there
into prairie. How wet and blue, he
dazzled up like foam—I must, I must—and that
sea again, only
a word on a page to us, dense
and imagined as a fly's iridescent eye, but bigger.
Then upstairs once in the flat warm spring,
I opened Sandburg's book. "When water
turns ice, does it remember one time
it was water? When ice
turns back into water does it remember
it was ice?" Such a trade, as solemn as it was silly,
but I pictured a man
staring quietly into a glass
where ice of no consequence suddenly weighed more
than the world. It was my mother out back—
the *tink tink* of her spade—and the flowering plum
just releasing its small
bitten wealth, drifting out
past the alley, too high, yard after yard.

THE BOG

When you came north that spring, we all
got out to look for moose, roads
loopy as orbits in a star book,
and ended at the bog. Our car door
cracked its dead weight once, twice, three times
until the four of us slipped out, our kid
just a little kid but serious about quiet.
We followed out as far as water
bluebells and bouncing bets, Jack-in-the-Pulpit in its
striped pajamas sleeve, and sat so still
we could have been stumps, less and less
as minutes passed
anything we remembered being.
Every time we heard a splash
we turned, all of us, *as if, as if*, but it was
simply bird or fish eager
to get at it. The low buzz of something, the slow rings
of what was hidden but breathing in the water
made us slower until we nearly
buzzed ourselves as though the wish to speak
had sound. We heard crashing
in the woods; you looked up, hopeful.
We heard insistent calls of crows, and a voice
so sleek and brutal, a wolf, I thought—but awfully
far away, I whispered to my son, who *shushed* me.
How long to wait? We'd heard there was a whole
moose family there—mother, father,
little mooslings (is that how it's said?)—and out they'd come
at suppertime if we were quiet. We were, I swear,
that quiet. The buzz got louder
with every rising interval of quiet, which itself
seemed solid as a brick
you'd build with. How many bricks of quiet
make a house of quiet big enough to hide in? To disappear—
we wanted that—so the moose would come out happily,

nonchalant as any humming thing, that is, those things
that hum. Clearly not a moose. The things
one thinks of, sitting in a bog, alert
to happenstance, to marvels—O human vanity—as if
alertness were enough.

THE GOING OUT OF
BUSINESS GREENHOUSE

The old lady pauses above the register.
I think it's
forgetfulness or grief.
It's stuck, says the other right behind her.
They pitch forward
to see better—diggers
at some neolithic site.

Such a place, out on a dirt road. Chicory
floods the whole way there. This old thing, says one.
And they look at me
and my potting soil. The money feels
stupid in my hand.

They can't get it open. Well, says the other,
and sits down. The light
everywhere is green and broken. She begins
folding up a garden magazine to make
a fan. I think of those orphans out back: coreopsis
and balloon flower and the sullen somber rose.
We've killed off
most all the plants, the first woman tells me,
rather triumphant. The other is
nodding. She fans herself
wildly with the colorful bent page.

I see you're closing, I say lamely
by way of sympathy, some start
to it. Oh that, says the standing one.
It's just our habit, says the other,
the fan still blurring.
We're good at it, adds the first.
Good at what? Closing? Doing in the stock?
I wait for their laughter
to tell me. But we're done.

Hoes and rakes and trellises....
It's private as dust
in there.

INVENTING THE TRAIN

On the high trestle where lovers
abandon their romance, rolling it into muffled sounds,
its ghost whistle whine
tossed off the bridge: *to hell with you, Jimmy O'Brien,
you're just a jerk anyway*—like that,
the voice of the heart
rising at last above its nonsense.
So I imagined
the old train—finally wooed and loosened and emptied
by such failure—stopping for us
abruptly, like a sunstruck horse.
It was dark. I got on first
and pulled you up.
It took a lot of convincing until I dreamt
food for us in the gleaming dining car, and waiters
too young to know what they were doing.
They were that cute. They still
liked their jobs. And the hamburgers arrived with splendor,
relish rich, tomato and pickle.
By then you were eating and had that sweet
unpuzzled look. But the secret
I secretly invented
wouldn't stop inventing: the club car,
the sleeping car for later, all
the landscape from here to Massachusetts.
Trees were the hardest, their
miraculous detail. Faster, I whipped
the old train, faster!—
blurring them to a frantic pitch,
a belief, that quick. So easy
in those lovely manic days
to fool you.

THE MUSEUM

My father liked to lay his enormous body
before the mummy case,
first a joke, and then as habit
if being dead for centuries is habit.
He slept like that
while my brother and I moved
through the upper floors like fish
dazzled not by light
but by exquisite gloom, and stopped
before the diorama
where tiny cavemen, thick as only thugs
are thick, jacked up their
arms in fury. It was the women
who lounged about and scraped
the bison skins, amused or bored,
attentive to the detail. Two minutes—

then Eskimos, then Cherokee
and Sioux: those beaded dresses, leggings,
their dizzy color streaked
the tall glass cases, intricate
as arteries, and lush, the way things draped
to love the body. Dim in there,
always, and index cards
taped to glass, yellowed,
slightly curled.

Still my father slept and turned, his head
rolled back to elsewhere
while we watched the plainest bone change
and darken and not forget—femurs
into clubs, the pelvis of a bear splintered down
to its wicked needle life, set
as quills straight out to gouge an eye.
Yet human skulls

were sweet now, simply bowls
or spheres to aim at stars. My brother kept us
toward the mastodon, the ribs
laced high, the skylight blinding, a blurred box
those days it rained.

When it rained I thought:
my father will sleep for years like this.
Angels or ghosts, we thinned down
like a city shrunk to a cooking pot, a few
blue feathers on a stick, and flying.
This dream is childhood, this
and this: our father dead, we liked best
to walk backwards into those
massive rooms, thinking
the smallest voice—*now turn*.

SOCCER PRACTICE

The field could be all water, easily,
these children deep
in the trance of it, every rise of wave.

But I can turn my head
and turn the angle
of the water. The ball goes

crooked then, a funny arc.
They reach around
and sideways for it, a trick

they learned on land, not
a real ball—ha!
In truth, they kick and circle

and fall. September. This is practice.
And even the trees
are thinking about it—changing,

their red and yellow brilliance
no longer secret
in a couple of weeks.

Now it's too hot
for anything to change.
At the field's edge, the houses

look as sealed and still
as some
absent dream of houses, except

the gray boxes
rumbling out back, the stinging
metal ache in them

that cools
everything inside. This is
forgetfulness. A drug

and a perfection.
Then they shudder down to nothing.
From nothing come

the children quickly, out of breath
still calling to each other,
not drowning.

IN APRIL

Near the bike racks, a dog
is losing his mind, thinking—what?—
that life as a dog
isn't one big bone, days are short,
and memory is a complicated scent.

Believe this too: everyone
is cheerful—it's April—printed flowers
all over their corny short-shorts.
Up the street, another stand of trees, and another
and another on that high hairline.
Tree thoughts, straight
out of the head, though a little redundant.
But nothing's really in leaf. Limbs still sway and creak,
twigs in the buff: the mind's
a genie in its bone bare socket.

The dog keeps at it—sniffing.
I see right through to his ribs, through the ribs
to the soft parts, all order and pulse—
of course, the buried heart
where all dark liquid begins.

ACKNOWLEDGMENTS

The Massachusetts Review
"The Luxor Baths," "The Berlin Wall, 1966"

The American Poetry Review
"Distance"

The Virginia Quarterly Review
"Then," "The Kingdom"

Poetry
"Driving After Supper," "Rare Old Violins,"
"Ash Wednesday"

The Iowa Review
"The Stairway," "Geese," "On Sorrow,"
"The Crickets," "At School"

Field
"At the Y," "Walking Home," "The Boy Ghost,"
"Up in Air," "In April," "For Emily Dickinson,"
"Snow," "Inventing the Train," "Holy Cards,"
"Argument, With Migration"

Denver Quarterly
"Tree," "Town Pool"

Seneca Review
"Spring," "In Summer"

The Women's Review of Books
"Piano," "Winter"

The Gettysburg Review
"The Surveying Class"

Crazyhorse
"Work," "The Junked Cars"

86

The Southern Review
"The Bog"

Prairie Schooner
"Painting Ferns a Mile from the Stadium,"
"Dr. Williams' Desk," "For All Those Poets One
Reads in Childhood"

Northwest Review
"The Going Out of Business Greenhouse"

The Georgia Review
"Total Eclipse," "Moss Burning"

The New Yorker
"Maps"

The author wishes to thank the Ragdale
Foundation for the residency and the Center
for Artistic Endeavors, School of Liberal
Arts at Purdue University for the fellowship,
both of which helped greatly in the completion
of this book. Deep thanks as well to David
Dunlap and Berkeley Brown McChesney, first
readers of so many poems here. The poem
"Ash Wednesday" is for Leonora Woodman.

ABOUT THE AUTHOR

Marianne Boruch is the author of two previous collections
of poetry, *View from the Gazebo* (1985) and *Descendant* (1989).
She teaches in the graduate creative writing program
at Purdue University.

COLOPHON

The poems in this book were typeset in 11 point Garamond. This type was originally thought to be influenced by Claude Garamond's ROMAIN DE L'UNIVERSITÉ; however, many of the present-day versions of this type are based the the TYPI ACADEMIAE of Jean Jannon cut in Sedan around 1615. The book was printed on 55 lb. Glatfelter (an acid free paper) by McNaughton & Gunn in Saline, Michigan. Text and cover design by Carrie Andrews. Cover illustration by Jacqueline Boyle.